Symphonic Themes

I CAN
PLAY
THAT!™

Music Plus ♩
5 Michael Street
Kitchener, Ont. N2G 1L7
(519) 745-8530

Wise Publications
London/New York/Paris/Sydney/
Copenhagen/Madrid

Exclusive Distributors:
Music Sales Limited
8/9 Frith Street,
London W1V 5TZ, England.
Music Sales Pty Limited
120 Rothschild Avenue, Rosebery, NSW 2018, Australia.

This book © Copyright 1993 by
Wise Publications
Order No. AM91313
ISBN 0-7119-3564-5

Book design by Hutton Staniford
Compiled by Peter Evans
Music arranged by Stephen Duro
Music processed by Interactive Sciences Limited, Gloucester

Photograph courtesy of:
The Image Bank

Music Sales' complete catalogue lists thousands of titles and is free from your local music shop,
or direct from Music Sales Limited. Please send a cheque/postal order for £1.50 for postage to:
Music Sales Limited, Newmarket Road, Bury St. Edmunds, Suffolk IP33 3YB.

Printed in the United Kingdom by
Halstan & Co Limited, Amersham, Buckinghamshire.

BEETHOVEN
Symphony No.2 in D
3rd Movement Theme (Scherzo) 6

Symphony No.3 in E♭ (Eroica)
1st Movement Theme 10

Symphony No.6 (The Pastoral)
3rd Movement Theme 30

BRAHMS
Symphony No.1 in C Minor
4th Movement Theme 4

Symphony No.3 in F
3rd Movement Theme 14

DVOŘÁK
Symphony No.9 in E Minor
(From The New World)
2nd Movement Theme 36

HAYDN
Symphony No.97 in C
2nd Movement Theme 38

Symphony No.104 in D (London)
2nd Movement Theme 40

Symphony No.94 in G (Surprise)
2nd Movement Theme 46

MENDELSSOHN
Symphony No.3 (Scottish)
3rd Movement Theme 12

Symphony No.4 (Italian)
2nd Movement Theme 16
3rd Movement Theme 18

MOZART
Symphony No.50 in D
2nd Movement Theme 42

Symphony No.6 in F
Minuet And Trio 44

SCHUBERT
Symphony No.5 in B♭
2nd Movement Theme 22

Symphony No.8 in B Minor (Unfinished)
1st Movement Theme 34

TCHAIKOVSKY
Symphony No.5
Extract from Andante Cantabile 20

Symphony No.6 (Pathétique)
March Theme 24
1st Movement Theme 26
2nd Movement Theme 28

Symphony No.1 in C Minor
4th Movement Theme

Composed by Johannes Brahms (1833–1897)

5

Symphony No. 2 in D
3rd Movement Theme (Scherzo)

Composed by Ludwig van Beethoven (1770–1827)

Symphony No. 3 in E♭ (Eroica)
1st Movement Theme

Composed by Ludwig van Beethoven (1770–1827)

Symphony No.3 (Scottish)
3rd Movement Theme

Composed by Felix Mendelssohn (1809–1847)

Moderately slow

Symphony No.3 in F
3rd Movement Theme

Composed by Johannes Brahms (1833–1897)

Moderately

Symphony No.4 (Italian)
2nd Movement Theme

Composed by Felix Mendelssohn (1809–1847)

Symphony No.4 (Italian)
3rd Movement Theme

Composed by Felix Mendelssohn (1809–1847)

19

Symphony No.5
Extract from Andante Cantabile

Composed by Piotr Ilyich Tchaikovsky (1840–1893)

Slowly and with feeling

Symphony No.5 in B♭
2nd Movement Theme

Composed by Franz Schubert (1797–1828)

Symphony No.6 (Pathétique)
March Theme

Composed by Piotr Ilyich Tchaikovsky (1840–1893)

Symphony No. 6 (Pathétique)
1st Movement Theme

Composed by Piotr Ilyich Tchaikovsky (1840–1893)

Symphony No. 6 (Pathétique)
2nd Movement Theme

Composed by Piotr Ilyich Tchaikovsky (1840–1893)

Gracefully

Symphony No. 6 (The Pastoral)
3rd Movement Theme

Composed by Ludwig van Beethoven (1770–1827)

31

Symphony No. 8 in B Minor (Unfinished)
1st Movement Theme

Composed by Franz Schubert (1797–1828)

Moderately

35

Symphony No. 9 in E Minor
(From The New World)
2nd Movement Theme

Composed by Antonin Dvořák (1841–1904)

Symphony No.97 in C
2nd Movement Theme

Composed by Franz Joseph Haydn (1732–1809)

Symphony No.104 in D (London)
2nd Movement Theme

Composed by Franz Joseph Haydn (1732–1809)

Symphony No.50 in D
2nd Movement Theme

Composed by Wolfgang Amadeus Mozart (1756–1791)

Symphony No.6 in F
Minuet And Trio

Composed by Wolfgang Amadeus Mozart (1756-1791)

45

Symphony No.94 in G (Surprise)
2nd Movement Theme

Composed by Franz Joseph Haydn (1732-1809)

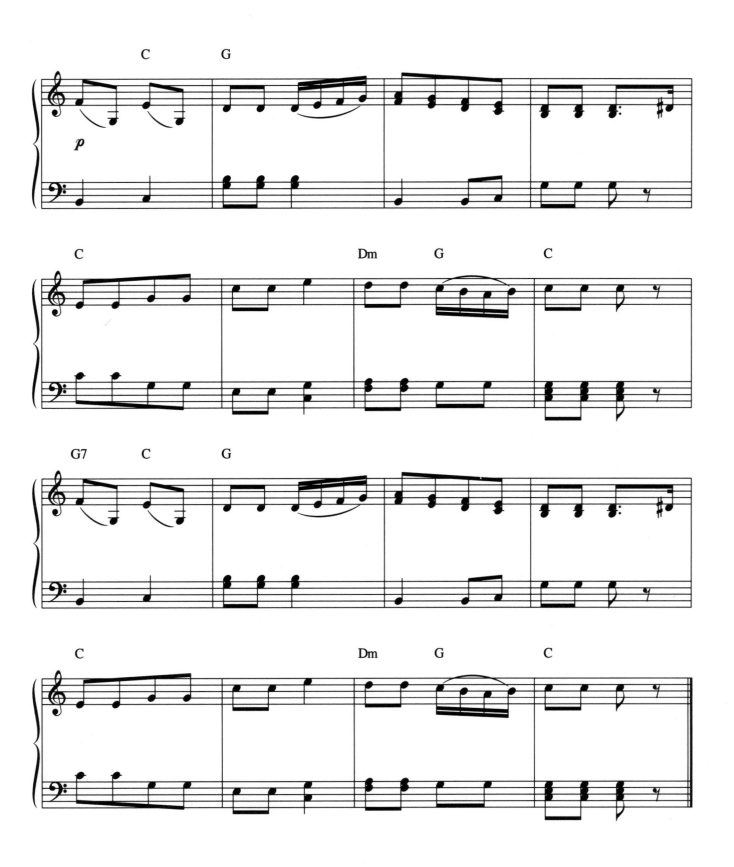

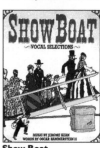